A Blue Beyond Reach

8/12/04

J.B. —
My favourite
restauranteer. Enjoy
the book!

Best Wishes,
Sean Dutt

A Blue Beyond Reach

poems by
Gaar Scott

The Muse Rules
Indianapolis

Acknowledgements

Gratitude to the following journals and anthologies where some of these poems first appeared:

—Aethlon: The Journal of Sport Literature: "A Warmth of Waters", "Like a Strange Pair of Wings", "Another Reason for Scales", "Across the Lake"
—Arts Indiana Literary Supplement, 1990: "Shellfish Reaction"
—Bellowing Ark: "Someday", "For Something In It", "Ceremony of the Two", "April Alone", "For Micki at Seventeen", "Wedding Gift", "Somehow in the Sonata", "In Autumn Breaths", "In the Ice and Mist", "Love Seems A Bird", "Alleys Like This"
—Celebrating Life: Anthology: "Toni the Dancer"
—The Flying Island: "Father's Day, June 21, 1998", "Snow Dream", "That Part of the Land in Me", "For Barb", "Goddamn, Grandpa", "A Trio of Oyster Pirates"
—Free Songs: Anthology: "Like Gauguin, I Mean"
—Gypsy: "Burn the Silk Ones"
—The Literary Review: "Across the Street"
—The South Carolina Review: "Veal"

Cover Art by Gaar Scott

All Rights Reserved.

Copyright © 2004 by Gaar Scott

The Muse Rules: a literary press
715 Northview Avenue
Indianapolis, IN 46220

ISBN 0-9713615-0-9

Table of Contents

Like a Strange Pair of Wings	3
Veal	5
A Trio of Oyster Pirates	6
Across the Street	7
Like Gauguin, I Mean	8
New Unsettling Ways	10
Father's Day, June 21, 1998	12
Spring Sign	13
Another Reason for Scales	14
Love Seems a Bird	16
Blue River Blues	17
Goddamn, Grandpa	18
All I Can Promise, Anne	20
A Kind of Pain	21
A Christmas Poem	22
Snow Dream	24
For Barb	25
One for the Boys in the Old Neighborhood	26
One Sharp Note Short	28
Burn the Silk Ones: Neutron Bomb	29
Sharp Talk	30
Wedding Gift	32
Only the Rhododendron	33
Someday	34
Alleys Like This	35
April Alone	36
To Loudie Sloane Wherever She Is	37
Anymore	38
Suicide Note	40
The Browns Stirring	41
The Cottonwood at the End of the Street	42
Summer Goodbye	43
That Part of the Land in Me	44

Somehow in the Sonata	46
Our Blue Dance of Love	48
I Begin to Love	50
Into the World	51
Friends	52
Jesse Shall Be a Tree	54
Did You Ever Feel This Way?	55
In Autumn Breaths	56
For Micki At Seventeen	58
Like Any Other Walk up the Street	60
Middle Class Nightmare	62
Upside Down	63
For My Sister	64
Ceremony of the Two	65
Resting Her Elbows	66
Important Things	67
A Turn of Adam	68
Maple Syrup Blues	69
You Would Come Home	70
Hunger and Light	72
Shellfish Reaction	73
I Might Be of Some Help to You	74
Toni the Dancer	76
In the Ice and Mist	77
Across the Lake	78
July Air, 1957	80

for Edrie, my mother

Special Thanks

A special thank you for the following people without whose patronage this book would have been impossible:

Anita and Erik Chickedantz
Gayle and Doug Clark
LeAnn and Bruce Davis
Betsy and Tom Hollo
Linda Hunt and Tim Morrison
Deb and Neil Kobi
Dianne and Greg Leatherman
Darla and Hunter Leggitt
Debby and Dave Lehman
Kim McDonald and Dave Brumm
Jamie and John Michalski
Christine and John Patten
Bill Raftree

Like a Strange Pair of Wings

You will heartshoot
his remaining Springs
from a hundred yards away—
just below the timber line
belting the horned
mountain's side.
Echoes from the gunshot
crashing him—hindquarter
and snort—into the clover,
will resound throughout
nearby gullies and mounds
like an eerie Taps.
You will gut him yourself.

Like a strange pair of wings,
his rack will soar
above the fireplace
in what was, before, your den.
The epic of the quest
will edit itself, chop
and roast itself and its parts
down over time.

After wallpaper and paneling
changes in the den, you will move
the atrophying antlers
up inside the loft
alongside other trophies
of the trail. You will
notice the velvet

at the center of the mount
has darkened to a blood-
like hue. One night
you will be found
sleepwalking in the attic.

Your hair will whiten—
fade to a paleness
near the shade of a buck's tail.
Older, you will daydream
through frosted windows
on dried, winter Sunday afternoons—
secretly yearning for
a return of the bones
disguised as a deer.

Sensing a hunt again
beginning, you will start teaching
your grandchildren painting
and music. And one unexpected Fall
morning around feeding time,
an inky pool forming in
your granddaughter's love-
filled eye, will clear
an old hunter—one once
too young to know
a hunted deer never dies
alone on a mountain.

Veal

I do not know every
chemical or metal nuance
haunting the life and death
of the veal chop atop the grand
china plate before you,
but they were not pretty.

The exact mechanics
chorusing the calf's final moments
escape me, as well.
But I am aware this candy-eyed
four-hoofer probably waltzed
away its last steps
to the melody of a meat cutter
humming to himself—
maybe to forget the slaughter-
house score.

Later, I, the violinist
in the bistro serving
its marinated muscles, will send
rhythms of romance
through rooms of well groomed types
like you feasting on the sauce
covered ligaments and sipping
chardonnays amid one hour long
discussions of the Market, Trade,
and always War somewhere.
But I always bury in the "piece
of the day" the tune of that meat
cutter trying to forget.

A Trio of Oyster Pirates

Much like the Spring day's
sunlight spicing up the platters
of fettuccine, Barbara, Alexis, and Carrie Anne
would blossom into the bistro
stopping only for assistance
from the head waitress,
whose reservation chart
guarded the mouth
of the pour of tables.
Barbara, Alexis, and Carrie Anne
would slow for the sights
seasoned across the gumbo
of faces and foods. And like
a trio of oyster pirates
clad in stolen silks,
they'd wind between lobster
and lobster bisque, settling
at last in the roundtop
oak harbor where pasta
twirled right and fancy
wordplay among friends
culled more than one bad
blue crab or claw of gossip
before it was swallowed
too, too deep. Occasionally,
a red lipsticked white
wine glass would offer itself
to the wooden floor.
After desserts and a quick look
around, they would leave.
Some days, the right soup
spoon left with them.

Across the Street

I watched from my front porch
as the young bipolar approached his car,
wrench in hand, to tear it apart, completely.
He wrestled with the bolts beneath,
laboring under the sun's rays
blasting skin and steel alike.
Braving oil stains and grease, stones
and dirt, he was not just
doing it for fun. No, the lithium kid
was doing down demons
at every screw turn.
The engine and transmission full,
top-heavy, bottomed-out with personal
challenges and fates taunting
him. His manic touch realized to the nth
degree every twist, every oil drop's
potential. Only the medication
he hadn't been taking would interrupt
the flowing labyrinth of his mind.
His brain swirled: did he really
just make shitting too complicated?
The sun wore on.
Finally, he stopped. Pulling himself
from under the car, he stood up, looked
around in my direction. As he headed
across the street to greet me,
he stepped in a dog pile in the grass.
Flies flew. Raising his arms like wings
to the sky, he began to laugh and laugh.
I did, too. The trees turned in the wind.
We stopped laughing.
The wind started up.

Like Gauguin, I Mean

Bought a hat said to be just
like my idol's—that escapee
from middle class humdrum to island
beaches and art—Gauguin's.
The ad declaimed I already had the soul,
all I needed was the sea-sotted,
sun-soaked, wind-torn hat.
I could buy it right now from them.
I used my golden credit card,
their toll free number.

My South Seas derby arrived
hand delivered on the third day
from calling. With my finest
set of carbon steeled shears,
I split open the wrapper.
Two inch square instructions
slipped out; next, my renewed life.

"Put the hat under tepid water.
After it is wet, fold it, twist it,
roll it. Create your own unique
shape." I set up my camera to take
"before" and "after" photos.
Click. "Before." Gathering all four
corners of my creativity together,
I strode into the bathroom and sank
my fingers into the sinkful of easy
brim and brine. Click. "After."

Beautiful. A seasoned cranium cover
as authentic as the copywriter
wrote it would be, straddled my skull.
The rebel part of Gauguin was on me.
I was Gauguin. Mystified, I wondered
how that catalogue company knew I felt
this way? Like Gauguin, I mean.

New Unsettling Ways

The fox squirrel spun,
tail turning
limp as a white flag.
The killer part of me
bolted in my .22
had hit him in the fullness
of his chest cavity.

Blood rushed around inside
him like ocean waves
sinking a ship.
Warm fluids
rushed to his throat
in new unsettling ways.

Shooting past branches,
leaves, with a bones-to-the-ground
"kertonk," he ran,
scrambling anyway
he could—his salvation
always a tree.

Halfway up an oak's trunk
everything stopped
in a sort of rest.
His eyes deepened
to full forest. He heard
my rifle click and footsteps
like I would not hear
certain streams of the wind rustle.

Nearly my height
on the tree side,
our eyes met blue to brown.
We stared too long.
I killed him quickly.
Years later,
I would seek his name.

Father's Day, June 21, 1998

I never saw so many red-haired
boys like you wanted
me to have, Dad, until
your ever bluing eyes were gone.
Your voice played back
from the pipes of the eternal
crowd. Your profile and back
of head, like seams in a quilt,
loomed from strangers in the right
light and angle. Your mannerisms
began invading mine.
My first Memorial Day
without you, I finally forgave
you your backhands at the supper
tables of my boyhood and tossed
a half dozen white roses
into the river
where your ashes
turned to silt—you always
called it, "Decoration Day."
Worst, you'll never meet her—
my someday her—and I fear
now neither will I.
There are still so many
of the world's broken strings
frayed like ones on
old discount store kites
left between us
for me to re-tie.

Spring Sign

She stood, broom in hand,
just beyond the morning fog
on her second-story airing porch
a lawn or two up the street.
I stood in my backyard
yawning, sipping coffee, looking.
Magnolias bloomed between.
She began to sweep.
I watched her body peekaboo
from behind the curtain of petals.
I heard her humming. Her notes
rounded slowly towards me,
turning about leaf and branch,
slipping into my ears.

Surely,
robins are the second sign.

Another Reason for Scales

Early morning largemouth bass flops
popped through the haze
as the fisherman worked the shoreline
splashing lures
into the lily pads
nearly as loudly as the bass
catching his breakfast.

The angler saw bubbles
circle up through the still
waters around his bait
a microsecond before the trademark
jerk and swirl of the big
bigmouth bass.

Holding his prize up
by the lip into the sunshine
showed him another reason
for scales. Then the fish
fought clear to the stringer—
the fisherman loved the bass for that, too.

About to make his next cast, the sportsman
heard the call of his kidneys.
He stood up from his boat cushion
and turned to the back end
by the trolling motor.
Naturally, the wind picked up.
It was like being on roller skates.
As he fumbled for his member,
he never noticed the seagull

Spring Sign

She stood, broom in hand,
just beyond the morning fog
on her second-story airing porch
a lawn or two up the street.
I stood in my backyard
yawning, sipping coffee, looking.
Magnolias bloomed between.
She began to sweep.
I watched her body peekaboo
from behind the curtain of petals.
I heard her humming. Her notes
rounded slowly towards me,
turning about leaf and branch,
slipping into my ears.

Surely,
robins are the second sign.

Another Reason for Scales

Early morning largemouth bass flops
popped through the haze
as the fisherman worked the shoreline
splashing lures
into the lily pads
nearly as loudly as the bass
catching his breakfast.

The angler saw bubbles
circle up through the still
waters around his bait
a microsecond before the trademark
jerk and swirl of the big
bigmouth bass.

Holding his prize up
by the lip into the sunshine
showed him another reason
for scales. Then the fish
fought clear to the stringer—
the fisherman loved the bass for that, too.

About to make his next cast, the sportsman
heard the call of his kidneys.
He stood up from his boat cushion
and turned to the back end
by the trolling motor.
Naturally, the wind picked up.
It was like being on roller skates.
As he fumbled for his member,
he never noticed the seagull

that noticed part of him.
He had no idea gulls struck that fast.
They could. The jarring flap
of gate crashing feathers and beak
pain clear through his dick
awakened caveman fear and memory.
He jumped into the lake
with the gull in tow.
In a strange water wrestling match,
he fought to preserve his penis
and lung power.

He'd done nothing harder
than strangle a gull hanging to the end
of his schwanz, but he did it.
Exhausted, he prayed he wasn't
too far from shore. He wished
he'd bought life vests
instead of boat cushions.
He began to wish a lot of things.
He was afraid to feel for it . . .
The whole lake seemed to be
filling his blue jeans.
He could see the new trolling
motor just purring
as it pushed his boat
across the third basin.
His last thoughts
swirled with turtles.

Loves Seems a Bird

Like death. Great wings
fold about your words and steps
ensuring they don't fly away.
Prisoner of a sort, you breathe
in from the music around you
something deeper than its melody.
Returning to history's childhood,
you eat a meat served
from the center of time's scarlet
heart. Your eyes shine
as if cleansed by lightning.
Your spirit, red like the blood
that is your ticket
to this primal raree
of the soul, ascends
to a pocketful of blue
in the sky, where soars a purple
bird whose mere silhouette
draws out a part of you
you never lived before—that is
nearly too real.
And, amid the notes sung
by this bird singing
far above the treetops, rings
a diamond sharp, gathering
your scattered corners
together, calling out to you
to ask this lover to dance
in your voice
with murmurs of the eons in it.

Blue River Blues

More like gravy
than a river, the river named
after Saint Mary pours itself
across the countryside.
Like bubbles, inedible fish
rise through the skin
of its dross seeking
food and sunlight.
The Saint Mary's river is brown.

At midnight the brown river
turns black, slips on shadows
like a lace nightgown.
Old dreams of starlight
still haunt its ripples and depths.
The moon may shine in its belly.
The Saint Mary's searches
in currents of its own darkness.

Goddamn, Grandpa

I must have heard a thousand
times how you stood at one end
of a cornfield and shotgunned
at least a hundred rabbit-dinners
driven your way by all
of your sons starving
for a rabbit fry. I must have
heard a thousand times
how you blew
those rabbits' sides out
with number six shot, your blue
eyes bloodshot from bourbon—
goddamn, you were a man, Grandpa.
Your canvas vest sprouted
shells like a dictator's
does medals.

My dad, fifteen, once drank
a tin cup full of fresh-from-the-guts
steers' blood. The men at the slaughter
house laughed as he let it
oil down his chin, wanly smirked,
then belched it into the sun's
face. A sun that dried it—
tattooing his cheeks
so that as the day lingered, everyone
could see an authentic man
was strolling by.

I only wounded the first rabbit
I shot. It lay bloody in a briar,
just out of reach. I could barely see
it pump air in and out
of its chest. I stepped back,
and blew number six through its fur.
As that hare stopped moving, something
in me started—away from the tinny
badges of manhood so many of us
had trouble leaving behind, from
men who would pin them
to other men, from men
who would wear them.

All I Can Promise, Anne

Is one iceberg morning,
years from now,
you will tumble
from haystacked comforters
to place a toasty
right foot on frosty floors.
Strangely, no sudden chill,
no cut of cold
will sting your heel.
You will amble
to a porcelain sink to wash
night's curtain calls
from your eyelids
and brush your teeth
to go downstairs.
As your fingers
clutch the banister
to brace your now gray
body, dream-like, you will
notice a wrapped and stored
away memory of me
has been lightly dancing
before you, lightly,
as the aroma of coffee.

A Kind of Pain

Old Jimmy and I stood there
at the basketball game, fourteen
as could be, mentally undressing
those wonderfully fluffed, spoiled
cheerleaders from that school
across town we heard
had carpeted hallways.
We were marrying them, too,
in a distant, yet we believed
certain ceremony: we would be
driven to the church in our white
limo, step from its silk
and leather belly wearing
fine white top hats and tails—
smiling real toothy and sharp.
Then we would stroll lion-like
through the throngs of doting
fans, reporters, and our moms.

After memorizing those fourteen-year-
old feminine hips, Jimmy and I
would go to our homes for supper.
Later before bedtime, I would
step upstairs to my room
where I would lie on the bed
caressing myself—daydreaming
of those delicate, beautiful girls.
Mostly, though, I would just
lie there swimming in
a kind of pain
I still can't quite
describe or understand.

A Christmas Poem

He would hear Christmas
carols year after year,
Christmas mornings forever.

He would sleep his way
from steep sheets into blue
deep dreams of snowflakes
falling like icy spikes
through the pines' needles—
their very green. Arising
quiet as dawn's first
frost, he would kiss
his wife's pinked lips,
then shoulder his old army
parka—relic from another
age's polar bear war.
The night harboring
his night clothes promised
daytime of a sort.

As always, the first shoeless
step off the back porch onto the crusts
of Christmas Eve snowed
atop the land chilled his naked
soles—until he found the pond.
And he always found the pond:
perfect there in the darkness,
though not quite a circle:
no pure white ringing
nature's marriage into the rounds
sounding out its depths.

Ever more unsure, as usual, his
right foot advanced
into the stacked decay of leaves,
snapped twigs, wayward nightcrawlers,
rotted bluegill bellies, and perch
tails. Toes into muck swirls, he
descended over his temples
into the pond's December.

As his lungs forsook breathing
seasons of oxygen
for one long liquid inhale,
he would always hear
that dying of music
drowning men do—but he
would key, "Silent Night."

Snow Dream

Snowmen never leave the yard
and only the flakes and ice work
tell where the wind has been.

When a blizzard's breath explodes
so cold it liberates, when arctic
airs assault my neck
with claws that slice and soothe,
I begin to make secret partners
with the few
warmths there are in ice:
snowflakes to snowmen to snowpowders.

Thousands of fiercely truthful
white-faced moons linger
at the other end
of the universe: immortal images,
cosmic icicles testifying
like the last of Winter's snows
heated just enough to drool
down rooftops, then freezing
in a pointed, piecing way
to hang there—not quite bones.

In a snow dream, I float on,
cling to, slip from ice cakes.
Ice cakes—sweet, frozen, slick.
And all I can do
as I slide away, is scratch away—
leaving only tiny trails
into a primeval, glacial chill
with its own name for peace.

For Barb

Your night before surgery,
I want to summon you
over to my apartment.
There, I will show you
my paintings, pottery, books,
the sword on the wall.
I will describe to you
how spiritually significant
they all are—powerful.
Then, I want to be able
to tell you I have a secret
elixir stolen from a mystical
sect dwelling on top
of a remote mountain
in Java, and your
beautiful right lung
will not grow a stitch
of melanoma in it.
That you will get a call
canceling the operation.
The potion in your juice
will make you forget
all of this and you
can go home
on that tall red horse
I always see you riding.

One for the Boys in the Old Neighborhood

Bill did about anything mean
any kid anywhere could do.
He kicked the shit out of us
whenever his firehose-like
biceps chose to. From the fear
of his fists, we learned to lie
with eyeball-to-eyeball contact—
made a couple of us successful today.

Bill lived with his mother
through three beer-brained husbands,
two older, meaner brothers,
and an older sister
who was smuggled away
from all this emotional barbed wire
to a more teacup and butter knife
aunt, uncle, and neighborhood.

One drizzling Spring Saturday
morning, as I dribbled my basketball
around a corner of a street
I was about to travel in a new direction,
I saw a black and white police car,
red lights flashing, in front of Bill's
in-need-of-a-paint-job house.
"Good, they finally arrested
the son-of-a-bitch," I thought.
No, they were arresting, instead, his third
in a series of what would later be
called role models. Only
a week earlier, this oak-shouldered,
six-footer had driven up

in the biggest, most beautiful
silver semi-truck Bill boasted
any of us would ever see. Now
this moustachioed, ex-knight was
being summoned to appear
in a different kind of court.
Not quite knowing what to do, I stood
there with the ball between my arm and hip,
Bill's latest almost-a-parent did know.
He quieted himself enough to quiet
the cops. Off we went in all
our own directions.

Over the next few days, I told
as many kids as I could—legions of them—
about Bill's stepdad. I may have been
risking my front teeth, but I felt
in my dutiful way
that people must know the truth—
especially if it hurt Bill.
A week later I ran into him.
For the first time, Bill looked
me right in the eye
and with eyeball-to-eyeball sincerity,
lied his little ass off.
As he denied all the rumors,
I began to feel something new
in myself— a swirling dark part
that wasn't quite right, that reminded
me a lot of Bill.
We both stood there hurting
in ways we never even knew
we could. Later that night
we would both sleep, dreaming
for the first time flying dreams.

One Sharp Note Short

My love for you arose
quietly as if amid
gardens dreamed
by your eyes.

A sacred stillness
akin to that moment
lingering in a sunrise
before the lead
robin sings, piped
through—for the first
time I loved
both sides of a heartbeat.

Seasons later, you
and the words I wished
you to be, like whispers
mouthed into a snowfall,
left my life.

I told everyone
I no longer cared
for larkspur.

A secret horn of silence
would sound one
sharp note short, and
the purple pause
priming my heart
would diminish in ways
deeper than the pulse
of a teardrop.

Burn the Silk Ones: Neutron Bomb

so they finally
developed a weapon
setting only the flowers
on fire
well tell them to burn
the silk ones
decorating war memorials
everywhere
tell them
to leave the ones
on the riverbanks alone
their scents float free
their roots run
clear to the river

Sharp Talk

Early one January morning, I saw
old Billy—goateed, balded slightly,
and quite crippled on his right
side, swirl his broomstick
frame through the snow
storm slathering West Washington
Street. He was doing
his twig dance of flakes and gusts
as only his withered right
arm and leg would lead him.
Winter itself was no more
determined to reach the downtown
YMCA where he worked.

After arriving he, like
a one-handed athlete,
perfectly wiped the steam
from his glasses, stashed his coat
and muffler, then limped
to the locker room to pick up
not quite used up soapbars,
dirty towels, jocks, socks,
and shorts for laundering.

Bawdy sneers, greetings, tales,
and jokes welcomed him.
Joining right in, his face
sparked with sharp talk of Las Vegas—
where he and his savings account
would go a couple of times a year.

There he would find those beautiful,
two armed and legged, wondrous
women like he could never find
in Wichita. He would come
into them sweet and deep,
full of the right part of Hell.

One trip to Vegas
he never returned.
He won a fortune
at the crap tables,
married a show girl,
and moved to Florida.

Wedding Gift

This hand-honed, crafted-oak
kaleidoscope of flower
petals, flotsam flakes, and glass
glancing askance backwards
at you from its one end; pedestaled, and
prized for its contrasting,
complicated colorful patterns;
now graces your lives and living
room due to me, my clients,
and the art museum shoppe.

This special instrument
of endless spectrum and precise
design, dares to be presented
as a conclusion to every tiff,
quarrel, battle, war, and tear-
your-throat-out murder
between you two.

Immediately upon the finish
of brass knuckled words
and boxing gloved scowls, you
should pick up this kaleidoscope
and eye its symmetric splendor
for as long as you please—
becoming soon bored
with the relentless, dried
perfection; turning instead
back to each other
with the prayer of humanity
you are and are becoming.

Only the Rhododendron

Only the rhododendron loving
moonlight on the other side
of the screen opening
our bedroom life
into the night, knew
when one of our passionate
breaths choreographed itself
into a love dance:
reds reddened, greens,
blues, yellows swirled.
Purples turned
inside purples inside
stars inside stars,
churning into a sea
deeper than music.
Our love, once aware
of itself, leaned tenderly—
full of itself—over
our valleys' blueberries,
kissing their skins—
burying the ensuing
intensity between mountains'
thighs spread everywhere

Someday

Someday a promise will drift
into town and not be a gunfighter,
not be a built-for-action-type
with a faraway look
to his eyes.

He will not be out to marry
the most beautiful woman
in the county, or be in need
of just the right church
to turn him around.
He will not be here to turn
brother against brother or
mother against daughter.

He will laugh a lot, cry when
he has to. He will certainly not
fill a uniform or sport an office.
He will never descend
from the sky with trumpets
blaring. He will simply
arise in our hearts
like he's been doing
since dandelions.

Alleys Like This

The one-hundred-four-year-old
brick alley sprawls
up its host hill
like a half-submerged alligator.
At dusk, streetlights' askance
glows, like wayward cousins
to lightning, pool
into strange oases
on the worn grid of the handset
passageway. When it storms
the unevenness rounding the edges
of the clays shines dewdroplike
lanterns into the glosses
lacquered by passing thunderheads.
Antique alleys like this
help hold an old edge
for a neighborhood—for something
in it that might sing.

April Alone

aprils rains
like no other months
may touch off
tears from a part
a parsec away
inside

a corner
of you may die
uniquely
for all time

early flowers
dying in late
spring beckon
in their never to see
summer ways

watery eyed
big breasted april
promises tulips
clinging vines
green mornings
for your lonely
soul alone

remember remember
burn it into your roses
april is drunk
on nearly everything

To Loudie Sloane Wherever She Is

I first heard the name Loudie Sloane
cast offhandedly by her eighth
grade art teacher
between plum wine and potstickers
in a Chinese restaurant.
As she described Loudie's
storklike gait and open grin,
I promised to use that
name in a poem someday.
And it always pleased me
later how Loudie lingered—
poking her consonants and vowels
around my corners
providing music to whatever
moment she appeared.
Loudie's syllables sounded
bugles that signaled where
my true nouns and verbs
were bent. Second cousin
to the tap of a maestro's baton,
her nuances rolled through
the pipes of my imagination,
and tuned my metaphors.

Anymore

Anymore it's not
that easy.
You may not go
off to a garden,
soak yourself
in stars, dine
on sunsets and verses.
You will not be served
a supper of choice
accompanied with
dear friends.
It will never be
that easy again.
There is no
way they will let
you parade down
the street.
All your challenges
and problems will
not be draped from
one carved cross
from which you can
hang only once
for all the damages
and dangers you
alone stand accused.
These days you must
die with your humanity
sticking out of the bag,
your screams and moans

drugged into whimpers.
You cannot pass
gracefully. There will
be silk flowers
at the bier.

Suicide Note

A psychic muck, like an octopus,
slithered into my life sensing
which tentacle to attach
to each tender part.
At first, the squeeze
was like the handshake
of an old friend, almost smiling—
there seemed real choice.
Then something seductively eerie
started ringing
through my synapses.
My id collapsed into itself.
My blood was in total revolution.
Forever sort of hesitated for questions
then poured all over me.

The Browns Stirring

The browns stirring
in your eyes
could have dreamed
darkness
into being.

Your sway
full of right
hip and denim
draws everything
I am to places
you need
me and you.

Chalky legends of solitude
story your hair.
A far off purple
haunts your mouth.

Cupid's dandelion-dipped
arrows shoot
rhymes of thunder
into nearly every one
of your lonely
songs to Spring.

You are the red lipped, first-
lighted beat of sunset.

The Cottonwood at the End of the Street

The cottonwood at the end
of the street knows
sadness. Tall, it absorbs
early morning rains
clear through leaf and branch.
This cottonwood's mystery
looms amid its limbs, it must
reveal itself slowly,
it grows only slowly—not
possessing luxuries
like supple wrists or limber
knees to retrieve
a money clip or an errant twig
dropped. Realizing to the rings
the things of its life
causes this tree to be
only what it is,
everything it is.
Since a sapling, it has studied
the ways of the wind
and struggles skyward
after a blue
beyond reach, always.
Stretching with the inexorable
pain of a purposefulness, it can
cry no tear for the hurt
inherent in growth.
Lastly, this cottonwood
will turn into itself
then the whole of the forest.

Summer Goodbye

Monday morning, last, an old
irishman in Lincoln, Nebraska,
sort of awoke a lot like the young
man he used to be
in the Great Depression,
after fighting the night
before in an event the spectators
called boxing. This time he arose
like a harmony into the magpies'
cries, and stepped from the ring
forever – bawdy, bareknuckled
like one of his stories,
certain and silent
as a blackberry's sheen.

That Part of the Land in Me

In Orville Scrivner's woods
beyond the corner of the creek's
turn just to the west side of what
we then called, "Fox Squirrel Bend,"
there is on certain mornings, early
in hot weather, the Rising.
It is a veil of fog, dankness, and dew
that presses slowly skyward
through the dawn
draping itself from oak, sycamore,
and hickory. Straining sunlight
through its misty chambers, the Rising hints
at what hides in its shadowy hallways
as a more shy, nocturnal apparition
might. It is a given in Whitley County—
a ragtag mystery of smoke.

One afternoon in Mister Burson's
sixth-grade reading class, that part
of the land in me most in love
with secrets, pondered its way
into the Rising. As sun rays skittered
across the wooden floor, my adolescent
musings stirred into the enigma
of Whitley County. With feelings
a lot like suspecting a ghost
in a darkened room, I imagined
this wisp of the lowlands beginning
to shed layer after layer
of diaphanous silks—singing
mystic purity into the blood

in my veins; disturbing me
into the dark truths
found in merely being unable
to answer a question.

Somehow in the Sonata

To open up your insides,
you must fall in love
with those shadowy roses
blooming deep
in the forest—blossoming
untended in the eternal
Spring of unrequited love.

Music, silent as the center
of a stone, lives
there between
syllables of affections
unspoken. Lolling
about in that emerald meadow
allows a gentle pain
of peacefulness to slowly
acquire you: slip itself
across your shoulders
like an oversized cloak.

Then, somehow in the sonata,
soulful solitude becomes
enough. Like a plant,
you begin to need
only love's light
for your life. You explain
to caretaker friends
you are all right, you just
haven't met anyone
in a while.

You almost start
to believe it yourself;
believe you would be happy
as a plant—as a rose,
alone in a forest, terribly
untouched, living on light.

Our Blue Dance of Love

Long ago, pyramids ago it seems,
we began our blue dance
of love turned around
into emotional knee twists.
Being brother and sister it was
easy—father taught us.
You were beautiful, too.
Blue eyes seated amid mountains
of curly red hair—a backdrop
for your passions.
You were such
a threat to the myth
every oldest son is weighted
down by—a ball and chain
of outrageous expectations.
You were not quiet
about it either like little
girls should be.
You were disgustingly strong.
I hated you for it.
Your flaw was you loved
him and me both. There we were—
a ménage à trôis of family rage,
hurt, and turmoil. We learned
to love the combat.
We began to seriously
hate ourselves. We had become
the steeled, carefully tooled
children of stonewalled love.

Psychiatrists later, I reach out to you.
I think to myself, "At last,
we will step across the sibling side
of the dance floor."
Holding out my hand, I bow to you
even though you don't quite
believe it. You curtsy, smile,
and start to the ballroom
of our lives. As you turn and put
your arm about my neck, you begin
to hum the only song you know:
our melody of clear blue tears.
You sway with a type of childhood
innocence as you start to carve
out my heart, ventricles and all.

I Begin to Love

Like an early morning
encounter with violets,
a brush against
your lip too red
for friendship
leaves an aftertaste
of mystery.

Your fingers on my wrist
impregnate me
with a longing
only my body
across your small belly
could fulfill.

Quiet as the rose
that could be your smile,
I begin to love.

Into the World

Unlike a morning glory, the true
poet-warrior opens and opens
as day grows to night.
Working his humanity
into the world, he shines
with an afterglow of mountains
long vanished into myth
and sand. He is half-brother
to lightning whose
incandescence fires the many,
or few, who walk
alongside his aura of creative
power. His words
bring forth enchantments
from others which he whispers,
shouts, tricks, laughs,
sings, dances, or writes
into them while they
blossom into an army
marching in step with dandelions

Friends

Arriving first at the sushi bar,
I noted the wood—tables, booths,
chairs, and floors—nothing
permanent like marble or brass.
I instructed the waitress
not to seat us in a corner booth
because I suffered from a shellfish
allergy, and feel somewhat
cornered in a sushi bar anyway.
You were meeting me after
your dialysis and probably
felt a little cornered, too.
Old friends, we would swap
stories and jokes, talk
about changes in our industry,
how forward in time
is not always progress.

My melanoma was in retreat
now six years, my diabetes new
but under control. Each of us
was ducking cuts of the scythe.
We hadn't lunched in months.
As you peeled a shrimp,
I speculated how its juices
might spew onto my tuna tartar.
You mentioned your blood
pressure falls after treatments,
then turned away. Beginning
to sweat, you needed to leave.

You threw money on the table,
grinned, and were gone.

I lingered just to be near
people in case of a reaction.

Jesse Shall Be a Tree

A young runner's golden afternoon
in Nazi Germany
still glimmered in the summered
raspberry hues
bunched up in the pupil-blackness
lighting her face, her
ebonied grace, as something
of Jesse Owens' black
ran off the looping
autograph I was trying
to sell her, the one
mulberried into time.
Broke as she knew I was,
she was not about to let
money ensnare me
into this type of sale.
For to her, Jesse shall
be a tree, and the tree
shall be a book, read
by folks to free up
each others' blossoming
secrets of themselves.

Did You Ever Feel This Way?

Every time I gag
on a forkful of chicken
or sop of gravy, I
blame that old wolf
somewhere in the caverns
of my ancestry.
There has to be a lupine
influence there,
but I inherited only the bite
not the swallow.
All the while I'm gulping
vittles, I profess
love for the subtleties
of the sauces and herbs.
My early asphyxiation
will come as no surprise
to me, this style
of strangulation always
warns you with little
dry runs. One day, I
will over gorge my endless
mouth at a party, or alone,
and be unable to dislodge
the blockage halting
my life's air. I will expire
with blue eyes popping and lips
drooling sure as if
I had hanged myself.

In Autumn Breaths

The peak clears itself away
from the hill
as new growth thumbs out
high alongside a bank
of the lake. Treefuls of
October unleash in that way
only October has
with the winds,
becoming your morning prayer.

Mute, anonymous currents,
like the basin's first
cousin the river, turn
in autumn breaths
to soar straight up
the weathered cliffs right
through your clothes.
As if from an altar, you
are now enough
to look back into the thirsts
and hungers mouthed
by the boil of waves.

Yellows, oranges, golds, and
mysteries in distance
to the other shore, no longer
lift old dreams of wings
into your life again.
Your ear becomes absorbed
by the pillows of silence

propping the bent-winged
flight of a nearby seagull.

Someday, ancient promises
will step through
an eye of the gull

For Micki At Seventeen

Micki, remember, the first
rainy Spring afternoon
each year
wet with the world's tears
of rebirth can always
be for you
if you just open to it;
can be a seasonal icon
to those times
your solitary footsteps
trod along the sandy
paths of your most
personal nooks and streams.
To moments when you were
so lonely with yourself
you shared thoughts
with no one
except maybe a nearby
oak or hobo butterfly.
Take up that first storm
of Spring into the inward
searches of your nomadic heart
caught in itself—
shining with mysteries, brimming
with truths. And, carry
a purseful of thunder
into that feeling of a longing
for something only
a life's living can reveal—
that tells you
there is a part of you

worth waiting for, that somehow
lives or will grow, in
that deep part of you
you call your heart—a piece
of you that is as sure
as Spring to arrive,
and as greening.

Like Any Other Walk Up the Street

Sounding like any other walk
up the street when he phoned,
the Colonel told me
to round up my enamels and brushes,
go to Hangar 4 to the guarded
bomber there and letter
the name on it exactly
under the pilot's window
along the nose tip.
Then, shifting into a true
Colonel's baritone, he added
after spelling out the name,
it had to be done today
because the plane
would be taking off
tomorrow at sunrise.
I eyeballed my supplies,
picked the right
colors and bristles
and broke out
like my stripes in the war
allowed towards the other
end of the airbase.
Half-way, I stopped
by a latrine and spotted
the B-29's pilot humming, combing
his hair in the mirror.
Not thinking anything
about it, I peed, then
started on to Hangar 4.

There, I apprised the six-foot-four-inch
MP on duty with a rifle
to his shoulder and fixed
bayonets in his eyes, I was there
to paint the name
(I paused to look at the paper)
on the nose of the Enola Gay.

Middle Class Nightmare

To cook a middle class
chicken, you must
first awaken it
at three o'clock
in the morning.
Fill its head
with guilt and self-
doubt. Stuff
its latest nightmare
with a tale of tatters:
of poor sick people
loaded up on booze,
drugs, or pure mental
illness who hang out
on street corners.
Spice it up
with the unappetizing thought
that maybe these people
could succeed
and own a Mercedes,
but they don't
like the upsucking
way to the top.
They would rather lie
lifeless as a coney dog
in the gutter
than sell themselves
like a french fry.

As this chicken tosses
and turns, it will slowly
start to cook
in its own juices.

Upside Down

In the men's room at work
the ex-bomber pilot
casually mentioned his life
thirty years ago.
He brought up his nightmare
where he is floating
upside down and naked
in a B-52 cockpit
with gaping eyes
schooling like fish
around him in black smoke
burgeoning from rice paddies,
village huts, and jungle trails
miles beneath bomb bay doors.
After more encounters in
the lavatory, the pilot's
dream, like an air force,
began invading mine—
those brown eyes he did
not see that he sees now,
I see. And oriental faces,
thousands, all ages, dead;
apparitions. They show up,
ask the wrong questions,
make introductions; they
come into my bed
between me and everything.

Bombs explode and explode,
dark flowers bloom.

For My Sister

You are there in the darkness
drinking yourself, and not in
your way. In its way,
the darkness is drinking you:
a darkness that's your father.
As in a kind of dream,
strange and blued, you kiss
his open palms with your
black and blue life.
Then his face reddens like
the bloody lip between you two,
because he knows, he remembers
how he beat your young music
with his ungloved hands while
flashing his pair of always-angry-
Irish blues. Now, you know
nothing except to return, blindly,
pain to whoever-gets-in-the-way.
Still, you war with him
in the old living room
of a house long ago torn down.
You war, mostly with yourself.
You are becoming your own scar.

Ceremony of the Two

Roses—red, silks—white,
veil the bride's many
violins as she begins
an old as violets
love dance down the aisle.
An ivory bodice puffs
up her breasts and curves her
hips promising
her petals to his stem.

Tuxedoed, he stands
at the front of the sanctuary,
and this day he loves
tuxedoes. As the organ
music rises, he turns
to see her the same way
a shepherd might have seen
his love an eon ago:
her holy strawberry moon-cycling
beneath her stomach's
silken prairies as she stepped
through a fold to trod
robe-wrapped, sandal-toed,
towards the village's
stone well to drink.

Like winds kissing
tree tops, the couple stirs
scripture as only the sacred
can. The day is theirs,
everything else—sideshows.
The two—older than light,
together again . . . again . . .

Resting Her Elbows

Resting her elbows on the edge
of the folding table
after Easter dinner, she clasped
her hands and counted the yard
strung with relatives
sort of like a heron might.
Not old, sixty-two or three, she
had kind of looked at me
throughout dinner with grimace
and lipbite. She leaned
forward preceding important
cargo—"You've never
had children, have you, Gaar?"
"No, I haven't."
"Well, Bill, my late husband, and I
were thirty-six on one
trip to Florida. Sons in high
school. Our lives set and settled
like chocolate fudge. On the third
moonlit night, our suits came off
on the other sides
of our lives. I looked right
through Bill at the stars and felt
there's a person waiting to be
here through us.
After I told Bill, we loved ourselves
out. Our third son, Sam,
was born eight and a half months
later. Try not to miss out
on that feeling, Gaar."
I smiled and nodded, wondering
about dessert.

Important Things

Around 43, that nub of aloneness
you and your friends
used to refer to as a happy
bachelorhood begins to slowly turn
like old cheese.

Beautiful women start
to see you more
like a eunuch uncle, a pal,
graying confidante. Your shoulders
and hips hold less
than your tongue
which now speaks
only of important things.
The temptation becomes
to trash affection
like a worn lamp, instead
to smile with a lipful
of fifty-dollar bills.

And danger is going off
with your psychologist's advice
into the desert of companionship.
Orgasms there are the potting
of a cactus and a long, dry walk.

A Turn of Adam

Perhaps the contours of deer
antlers against the horizon
first coaxed you to love
trees bereft of leaves, to see
winter's blessings as not only wind
sculpted snowdrifts but twigs
high in oak and sycamore
branches descending into trunks
and stitching shadows
across the temporary
tundra of midwestern frosts.
And there appears to be in
leafless trees, too, a turn
of Adam that seems
to let you know the garden
will always be there
even in the slumbers
of December, the day-
dreams of January.

Maple Syrup Blues

Incantations whispered
over us as babes
rhymed our sleep
deep into the crib.
Maple syrup words
poured like storm cellar molasses
to sweeten the first
swallow of new sours.
Yet even the infants we were
heard the big, blue bruise
behind the eye and lip
lie—love can, indeed,
leave, and pain old
as salt, primal as a grizzly's
wail, will moan – boil up
from our ocean's bottom
to shriek to a high howl,
and like a straw
thrown by a tornado
pierce our night and day
dreams through to the headwaters
of all our tears.

You Would Come Home

Dad, you would come home
to the tender looks of a small
town who knew stories
clear to the first grade
about two certain boyhood friends.
Faces full of, "You just
couldn't save him, Max,
you weren't there."
Or, "He carried the Tommy gun
and you shouldered the BAR
didn't you, Max? Together
you two might have made it.
Here, have another beer."
Perhaps, "Call me, Maxie, I lost
my brother. We could go
for a drive over to the mill
like we did in high school."
Then the messenger who delivered
the telegram was heard
to have said, "Frank killed
nearly a hundred soldiers
before they got to him."
"It's possible," you wondered
to yourself. You had killed hundreds
in your battlefield nightmares
of smoke and fire. And there
was always a turn in the fight
when you would look up
through a treetop to a blue
in the sky that would light

up your death all around you,
all around you ... they would
have to kill any man
that had killed so many of them.

Years later, you would recall
Frank with feelings akin
to your first love, except
for her there would
come another.

Hunger and Light

Fireflies slipping over cattail
tops twirl with later afternoon
gusts that help carry them
aloft into aged oaks and hickories
encircling the pond
like sentinels to guard
nature flush with its many
masquerades. From the cabin's
steps at dusk, you hear birds
seek old music; bullfrogs croon.
At dark, the moon discreetly
hangs out her lantern.
Night plays its woodland concert—
waltzing you onto the porch
swing. Asleep, dreams come
like brain whales—great
tossing phantoms
swimming you deep.

Whistles and yips
stirring from hunger and light,
coax you up and into
morning hazes
honeycombed with themselves.
Your second thought this day
is of breakfast.

Shellfish Reaction

You are at a sidewalk cafe sipping
Chablis, eyeing your lover in the
sunlight, totally unaware of the bit
of shrimptail in your salad. You
feel the grapes. Self-satisfied,
though not quite cocky, you assume
the roses beside your table. You
send your eyes around the street,
hardly noticing your lower lip
beginning to thicken—you believe
you bumped it earlier. Then your
throat dries to sandpaper. Your
stomach quakes. Arising rapidly,
you grab at your collar and tie
only to throw up on the table.
You sneeze. Your eyes tear.
Your nose feels filled with cement.
Suddenly you inhale deeply through
your mouth. It's over. You look
about, redden, then pay your
bill and leave. On the way home,
you wear your car as armor.
You sit in the back seat hugging
your lover in a brand new way.
Haunting the back of your brain is
the thought: *this is how it sometimes
comes*: sudden and sharp, disguised
even as a shrimp, too eager to wait
for years of butter or tobacco.
You relax, gaze across the driver's
shoulder through the windshield.
All the roadsigns begin to look alike.

I Might Be of Some Help to You

Both of us knew your middle-aged
breasts betrayed your lungs
and liver, but what kept
my twenty-six years from crossing
the street to visit you were my
boyhood memories of polio and rheumatic
Fever—hearing life out in the front
yard. I knew what a prison
the couch could be and how
light would fashion shadows
through the side windows
of your house on the living room
floor into fences and walls—
corrals of darkness to pen
thoughts in. I could visualize
your television on, a lamp lit,
maybe a magazine or two
on your coffee table arming you
for the inner life. Sometimes, I
would stumble onto you sitting
on the porch. You would always smile
and talk. One day you seemed
to look right through the hobgoblins
from my youth and said, "C'mon over
sometime, Gaar, I might be of some
help to you." I never went over.

Later that year, you died
like a summer rain.

A week after, your voice
surrounded me in a nightmare
like my childhood
and admonished, "You're still hearing
life out in the front yard."

Toni the Dancer

Though it was Toledo
and a block of flats,
it was like being
in New York City the first time
I saw her
doing flips and pirouettes
down the street
in black tights like
unemployed Broadway dancers.
Maybe a ripple or two
on the wrong side of chunky,
but she was beautiful.
I wanted to sing her on
her way, but my landlady
who knew her, smiled
like an iris would and intoned:
"Toni's going manic again.
Isn't she a star?
What a way to tell the world
you're ill."

In the Ice and Mist

I sat in my car at the edge
of a half frozen pond
mulling over the frosted trails
and landscapes of my past.
A city of Canada geese
flapped and honked about
in the ice and mist.
Much like residents in a Toronto
borough the geese preened,
flirted, and made talk.
Sounding out in their mother
music, stragglers would descend
through the snow and chill.
The fogged-in ensemble
parted the vapors in me
to a lost place.
Near dusk, a lumbering gander
rose like a ghost
into the shroud of hazes
and disappeared. I could
still hear his call
after he was gone—somehow,
everything I had been
seeking began seeking me.

Across the Lake

We were going fishing
as we had so many times,
but maybe now for one of the last
times—you were starting
to pass through the graying
processes, soon to grow into all
colors, years or weeks away—
unknown, but we were about to part.
We knew it.

I hated bailing the boat.
Even more, I hated a phantom
boat cover we never bought
because we needed a rite of pain
hooked into every ritual.
The dipping of the plastic
bucket became a sort of mantra,
lulling me into a consciousness
searching out roadsigns
of our past I could set
my feet and hands to.
I would dip and dip and dip.

After a few shoulder breaking pulls,
the motor jerked and coughed,
trembled like a new born calf,
then shook itself into a start.
Once on the lake, sunken
islands and hidden points
became tackle box sagas
of shiny bluegills and dark

bass hoisted from their particular
waters. And, as always, you
loomed behind every word.

You kept measuring for sizes
and depths in me
as well as the bass.
You sought assurances
you were the typhoon of a man,
or fisherman, you needed to be,
needed me to be.

Several casts later you paused,
hunched up your shoulders
like an ice fisherman
around his hole and growled,
"Someone had to be pretty goddamn
tough somewhere along the line,"
as if neither of us ever would be.
With all the love
those eyes still held for me,
I felt they were thunderstruck
you and I had brought
our lives only to here:
this used boat, late in the day,
and mostly legends and stories
about fish.

Across the lake, we heard
a largemouth splash.
I started up the motor.

July Air, 1957

Five bass heads, mouths propped
open by twigs, hanging on nails
hammered into the side of my
grandparents' white garage, dried
in the July air. Fish caught
by my grandfather lined up—
anglers' shrunken heads, evidence
of expertise with a fly rod.
My father and I listened
to the lowdown on each catch,
nodded and muttered praises.

After lunch, my family and
grandparents gathered on the patio.
Grandma told of new wrecked cars
towed onto a neighborhood
body shop lot, of teenage
blood and death all balled up
and collapsed into itself.
Later, my younger sisters and I
drifted over to the lot.
In the shimmying heat waves we
peered through the rent glass
and torn doors, and tried to grasp
in our youthful ways blood and
vomit stains from the victims
of lake country curves and hills.

Upon leaving, my dad and grandfather
smoked a last cigarette. My
mom and grandmother hugged.
My sisters and I tumbled
into the back of the car,
seat belts in our future.

About the Author

Gaar Scott resides in Indianapolis, Indiana, where he reads frequently at local poetry gatherings. He is a graduate of Indiana University in Bloomington, where he was also a campus activist.. He has supported himself mostly in sales focusing on television and radio.

Gaar is also an artist and has had work in the Indianapolis Museum of Art, and shows at the Arthur M. Glick Jewish Community Center and the Hilbert Circle Theatre, home of the Indianapolis Symphony Orchestra.

Gaar is a cancer survivor and like many poets has battled manic-depression most of his adult life. He struggled as a child with polio and rheumatic fever. His health problems have helped in giving him a unique view of life and creative impetus to his arts.